Behavioral Interview Questions and Answers

How to Face the Behavioral Interview with Preparation, to Relax, and Overcome the Job Interview. If You Know the Answers, the Questions Won't Be a Problem

HORATIO BIRD

Table of Contents

Introduction

We all dream of making our fortune, but very few are willing to go down the entrepreneurial path, face the perils, and take on any risk waiting here. This is why those people settle for the employee route, which involves providing services to a company, in exchange for remuneration. If you go this way, you also don't want to be in the same position your entire career. Everyone starts at the bottom, but it's up to you how high you can climb.

Times have changed, and the labor market is totally different from what it was 20 years ago. Everything is dynamic, competitive, and people are following their interests over the company. Our parents stayed in the same position for decades, and the salary they had was enough to support their lifestyle and put money into a property. They didn't need to take out a loan just to go on vacation, and they weren't using credit cards— at least not to the extent that we use them today—so they were able to manage income easier.

Building a career involves acquiring the knowledge and skillset to sustain a higher level of income. Searching for the ideal position can be very difficult, as every job looks good on paper, but it may not deliver to your expectations. When you want to get hired, you should aim high, while still correctly assessing your experience while applying. This is the central focus of what you should consider before beginning a job search.

We have to look after our best interests, so finding a work environment where we can grow and develop our skills, where we can learn more is another important factor. With that being said, the job market is competitive and the only way to stay ahead of the other candidates is to have an "extra ace up your sleeve." This means you will have to be overqualified, and have more insight and ability than the rest. If you can express these traits adequately on your resume and cover letter, you will have essentially stuck your proverbial foot in the door.

When searching for a job, you might think: "Well, I'll never know if they are going to call me for an interview." Curb this mindset because it won't pay off. As the population of unemployed works grows the chances of being scheduled for an interview are low enough as it is.. So why send hundreds of job applications, only to receive no reply, when you can send ten well-prepared, targeted interest applications and get a call back? You have to make recruiters believe that the job you are applying for is the only one you are considering, and your resume and cover letter will need to reflect that.

Customize these documents to highlight your specific strengths, education, and any training that can be linked to that specific position. This is nearly impossible when applying in bulk for multiple positions. Recruiters can spot a throw-away application instantly, and they will do just that. A curated job application shows you made the effort to analyze the position they need filled, are very interested, and won't waste their time.

By applying these tips, you're chances of being contacted by the hiring manager for an interview sky rockets, and this is where it can get complicated, as you then need to confirm you are a suitable candidate in person. It could be a pre-interview over the phone, where you need to be spontaneous, provide clear and concise answers to the questions, and be memorable as they haven't seen your face yet. If you leave a great impression, this step might secure an official in-house interview, or it could completely eliminate you from their pile of maybes.

It's all about delivering what you promised on your resume and cover letter. The hiring manager wants to find out more about you, discover if you are the person you are projecting on paper. You are more than likely that person, but emotions, mannerisms, and conversation skills might stop you from confirming it. They already have a profile of the candidate they are looking for in mind, and it's not a bullet point list of qualifications. They are not looking for a list; they are looking for a person. They are carefully analyzing your social skills and evaluating you as a good fit for the team and future asset for the company.

There are plenty of situations where a very qualified candidate didn't get the job because they didn't fit the profile the way the employer envisioned. They were hesitant, nervous, and altogether failed to confirm their ability to the interviewer. Let's face it, most of us have been the person in this situation who didn't get the job. And if you see yourself in this situation, you need all the help you can get.

Lucky for you, this book was written to provide you with tips and tricks, pivotal questions, and smart answers to prepare you for your next interview and land your dream job. If you are looking for advice, but also clear and concise answers to difficult questions, then this is the book for you. As you read through, you will find each chapter provides you with what you need to be ready for an interview, secure the job of your dreams, or advance in your current career. What are you waiting for? Your future awaits!

Chapter 1: What Is The Behavioral Interview

The hiring process in general can be challenging as a candidate, but also as an employer, who has to shuffle through hundreds of good, great, and so-so candidates to fill one position. As you can imagine, this is no easy task. Imagine finding a way to rank applicants will all different backgrounds and areas of expertise. General questions can lead to situations where the company representatives can't tell the difference between your application and the ten others on their desk..

This process may include a cover letter screening, a short pre-interview over the phone with the shortlist of candidates—both being eliminatory—and having an in-depth interview with their best options. Depending on the company policy, there can also be a few tests related to the tasks that will need to be performed when, and if, you get the job. The method most companies are using nowadays as a decisive tie-breaker when faced with more qualified candidates that al have about the same chances to get the position, the behavioral interview, and this is the method we will be discussing throughout this book.

In an average interview, you would talk with a future employer about what tasks you are comfortable with, and others you enjoy doing. The behavioral interview is based more on what you have already done. Words in this setting can be considered empty without examples, and the purpose of the behavioral interview is to provide examples of specific situations related to the tasks of the position you are applying for. By now, you probably already know how to ace general questions such as, what are your strengths, where do you see yourself in ten years, or what to say (and how much) when you are asked about yourself.

Every well-prepared candidate will know exactly what the interviewer wants to hear and will provide clear and concise answers to these questions. However, in this situation you are not being interviewed for a general position, and the interview is the perfect opportunity to prove that you are the candidate of their dreams. What better way to make your point than knowing the answers in a behavioral interview? Backing up everything you are saying with relevant examples, will allow recruiters to get to the heart of why you are the best match for the job.

Behavioral interviews best apply for more experienced applicants, but this doesn't mean that recent graduates will not face the same questions. The only difference is that they need to think about what they would do in a specific situation, so their answers are more hypothetical than empirical.

The behavioral questions are the most challenging part of an interview, as the questions are the most relevant to the available position. The experience will help you come up with the best answers, but it's up to you to highlight on the appropriate tasks or it will all be for nothing. This is no time to let your emotions take over, as there are plenty of experienced candidates that are losing themselves in these moments. Project confidence, be yourself, and highlight previous relevant tasks and provide clear examples.

Interviewers emphasize this part of the interview because they not only pay very close attention to your answers but your reactions while answering as well. Don't be afraid to provide details and examples to avoid vague and empty answers. The interviewer might pose questions in the from situations you will more than likely come across in this position, so they want to find out how you best handle them. You won't be able to predict every single question, but at least you will know what to expect. Being spontaneous and coming up with surprising answers on the spot may be a quality that is missing with the other candidates.

However, if you lack this quality, it doesn't mean that you won't ace a behavioral interview. The key to succeeding is preparation as we will go into more through the chapters. You will find the preparation tips you need, plus the most common questions you will receive in this part of the interview. After all, behavioral questions should be more about supporting your experience. Many experienced candidates look promising on paper, but they fail during the behavioral interview because they have difficulty conveying how much experience they actually have, what they have learned on their own time, and providing these examples to secure the position.

Remember! An interview is not an interrogation, as you haven't committed any crime and are answering for it in front of the police. The people in front of you are not the Spanish Inquisition, so you shouldn't feel intimidated by them. An interview needs to be a two-way conversation, in which you will need to speak freely, not to provide robotic answers (like following a script) for all the questions asked. While you may have a script for general topics, for the behavioral ones you can't provide the answers like reciting a speech. You have to use your intuition and anticipate these questions, so you can prepare for what's next. How? You will find it for yourself in the following chapters.

Chapter 2: Behavioral Interview: Why Companies Use It

You may be someone who likes to plan every aspect of life and expect it to play out that way; it's the unexpected that is usually the outcome. Who can honestly say they have never had a bad day at work? One of those days when nothing seems to be going your way and everything seems to be collapsing. This is what we experience when dealing with disgruntled customers, tight deadlines, or unhappy, irate bosses. You might also have an enormous amount of work to finish, and you can't decide which one has the highest priority.

All of these are the topics of the behavioral questions, and you can see why companies are big fans of this technique. General questions may not get candidates out of the comfort zone, and they easily remain calm and provide all the 'right' answers. In many cases, the general questions are not necessary, but most interviewers consider this part of the interview as "the prelude" for what's next. A less experienced, unaware candidate can fail here, so the general questions are still helpful for recruiters.

Your resume and your cover letter are just two documents that emphasize education and experience. These aspects are summed up here, and no recruiter will take them for granted. This is where the behavioral interview steps in, as these questions cover specific examples of your career that aren't discussed on your resume. To start, you assume the people in front of you don't know anything about you or your experience, and the behavioral interview is where you can shine.

If your work experience is diverse, you need only to focus on the relevant aspects, don't waste time covering your experience as a McDonald's employee or your first job at 16, when you are applying for a software developer position or senior accountant. The questions you can expect during this phase of the interview might start with "Tell me about a time when you had to deal with...", or "Give me an example when..." etc.

These questions are based on the competency required for the position. If you have done something similar before, you will not have any issues providing the right examples and pointing out why this position is basically meant for you.

You might be asked about when you had to deal with a cramped schedule, facing tough customers and how you won them over, or when you had to handle a load of urgent tasks, and you had to decide which one needed to be dealt with first. The employer is looking to see how you reacted in these difficult moments, so you provide the situation, the reaction and outcome. Some positions may have tasks and standards, that are difficult to deal with. In this case, you need to give examples that are close to the current job description. Here are a few to help you get a better idea.

Tough Customers

Any salesperson or customer service representative can relate to this issue as they are dealing with these situations in one way or another every day. The secret is to overcome these barriers and turn the outcome into your favor. Sales reps will always face people who are very difficult to convince. It can be a stubborn older person, who only thinks that the salesman is interested in taking their money. In such a situation, any point you are trying to make may not be well received.

However, if you are good at your job you can turn the odds in your favor and in the end convince this person to buy. Describe how you managed to win their trust, listen intently, understand their needs and any issues they have had in the past to break through to them. From a customer service representative point of view, this is the ideal situation in which you were able to calm down a disgruntled customer and managed to make a sale to someone who ultimately had no intention of buying that day and earning the respect and appreciation of the customer.

A Tight Schedule

Deadlines are decisive when it comes to pleasing your customers, and a company doing their best to deliver the project or product on time. The business reputation is influenced by the quality of service/project/product delivered, but also by the promptness of delivery time agreed upon with the client. You have more than likely faced situations where you had to work overtime, or weekends to make sure that the end product was sent on time. You can talk about a website, an app, or even interior design qualifies. There are plenty of examples you can provide in this case.

Too Many Urgent Tasks

It's hard to rank customers, as everyone should be treated the same, and one customer isn't more important than another. This is why you need a system in place to prioritize tasks according to their level of importance. The sooner a due date is, the more urgent that task is. You are responsible for planning and ranking these tasks, so in this case the interviewer is looking for an example of yours. Think of a day where the papers, and customer emails piled up; each one labeled "URGENT. NEED ASAP."

Some candidates are tempted to make up a story just to have something to say during this phase. Even when you don't have anything similar or even close to the tasks required for the position, you should speak from a hypothetical point of view and point this out to the interviewer. In this situation, they will appreciate the honesty. Therefore, the behavioral interview can be the perfect opportunity to score some points, even if you have no relevant experience at all. You don't have to be a know-it-all and you never want to appear taken by surprise or unprepared, as you should be ready for this section of the interview.

Chapter 3: The Best Behavioral Interview Preparation Tips

There is no person out there who can anticipate every single question and accurately provide the best answer — not even the most well-prepared and confident interviewee. The behavioral questions phase is considered the most difficult part of the interview when recruiters are looking to put you under pressure and see how you react. If you are feeling anxious about it, don't worry! This means that you care enough about getting the job, and most of the candidates feel the same way. However, anxiety and uncertainty are not something that you want to project during this interview, so you are probably wondering how to control your feelings, be calm and confident?

Your professional experience can be your biggest ally during the behavioral interview, as you are pointing out how you handled difficult situations from your own experience. A good story will win the recruiters on your side, and this can seriously increase your chances of landing the job. If you are a natural-born speaker, then you are a huge advantage, but you will need to make it sound sincere. These are some behavioral interview preparation tips:

- make sure to study the job description
- take a fresh look at significant projects/jobs/tasks you have previously worked on
- recall any previous job performance reviews
- compile a list of professional achievements
- when structuring your replies, use the STAR method
- honesty will score you points, as well as being open and loose
- practice your interview responses aloud
- make sure your answers are less than two minutes

Hiring managers want to find out how you behaved in an actual situation, the value you added to the situation (your contribution), and discover your perception of pressure at work as this is interpreted differently by everyone. They want to know about stressful, high-pressure situations you have worked in, to better understand if you are suitable for their staff.

The best source of inspiration while prepping for the behavioral interview is in the job description, and why you should know this part by heart. Find out all the tasks related to the job, all the requirements, and expect some questions related to these tasks. Now you need to extract the relevant parts from your personal experience and think about any and all challenging circumstances during your time. We all experience these situations, so I'm sure you can quickly come up with a few perfect examples. The key is to describe a difficult situation, what was your role in it, what was your contribution, and the result.

There are plenty of people who don't know how to pinpoint their most relevant experiences (although they have a few), and they get stuck during this phase. Practice is the key to learning how to control your emotions, to become more confident, but also to properly emphasize your skills, knowledge, and experience, and to provide examples for them. No answer will be considered wrong, as long as you can provide samples and arguments for acting and deciding the way you did. These are no "yes" or "no" questions, so you can take your time to discuss freely your previous relevant experiences. Your answer doesn't need to be a speech, so keep it short and concise, but still appealing for the listener.

These situations can be related to customers, colleagues, managers, or supervisors. One quality that is important for most candidates is emotional intelligence. This can be described as the art of understanding and expressing your feelings and emotions in a healthy way, while understanding the feelings and emotions of the ones around you. This quality will be discussed further in a future chapter of this book.

Your communication skills can help you during this phase of the interview, but it's highly recommended to structure your answers the right way. This is why many specialists would recommend the 'STAR' method to help you out with this issue. But what STAR stands for? S is for situation, T is for task, A is for action, whilst R is for result. You can follow this structure to elaborate on each response of yours. So, let's dig a bit deeper.

- **Situation:** You need to think of the context of your story, as you will need to explain to the interviewer when and where the event took place. For instance, you let the recruiter know that "I was working on the X project for a very important client..."

- **Task:** This is about your role in the situation. You bring in more details to backup the situation: "I was responsible for developing the interface of the new website...", or "for developing the mobile app for Android users..." According to the role or job you had in this situation, you can fill in the blanks and come up with the right answer.

- **Action:** This is where you need to get more specific and provide details about the task at hand. If we continue with the same software developing example, you can provide details of what you were doing: "using JavaScript for the site functionality, CSS for the interface, and so on..." Provide details on how you interacted with team members, management, and the client directly. As you will need to emphasize not just your job-related skills, but also your interpersonal skills. How did you act? What did you do? How did you cooperate with others to assure that the project meets your client's requirements, and delivered on time? These are just a few questions you will need to ask yourself when you are elaborating on this part of your answer.

- **Result:** What was the outcome of your actions? You can mention: "We successfully delivered the project on time, met all the requirements, but exceeded the customer's expectations. A month later, the customer came back to us with another project."

Now that you have all these aspects to consider let's set things in motion and sum up everything you need to prepare for the behavioral interview. First things first, you will need to go through the job description carefully. Write down the skills and qualifications mentioned in the job description, and think of a story that proves your capability in each area. But that's not all! Now that you know more about the STAR technique, you will need to write your own story (think of it as your written script), in which you will need to include all four aspects.

Do you know how actors are preparing for a role? They are rehearsing the lines they have to say. You have it all written down on a piece of paper, so now it's time to practice it out loud. The more you rehearse it, the more comfortable you will feel with your own stories, the more natural they will sound. As you will not be able to anticipate every question during the behavioral interview, it's good to come up with a strong set of anecdotes, to project confidence with every answer.

When you arrive at the interview, it's all about making a good first impression. Of course, being confident and providing concise answers will definitely score points, you will still need a lot more to convince the interviewers. They are not there just to listen to answers, they want to see your appearance, take note of your reaction to each question, study your body language, and the tone of your voice.

In terms of appearance, you need to make sure that everything related to your outfit and grooming screams professional and "I'm here for the job, when can I start?" People can often judge a book by its cover, so you will need to make sure your "cover" looks impeccable and worthy of a candidate with the right skills.

Men will need to pay extra attention to how they dress, as everything related to the candidate will have to project the image of the ideal candidate. Try wearing a conservative suit (pressed and cleaned), with a light-colored shirt (clean and ironed), a tie that goes well with the suit and shirt, with elegant, shined shoes. Oversize or flashy pieces can sometimes leave the wrong impression, so this is something to consider when choosing the right clothes.

In terms of looks, having a fresh shave, haircut, and generally put together exterior are a must. So pay very close attention to your nails, they need to be trimmed and clean, and leave no loose ends when dressing for the day, such as missed buttons or belt loops. If you are a fan of fashion jewelry, now is not the time for wearing them. Piercings, earrings, or anything similar should be removed if possible. Recruiters can easily be distracted from what you are saying, and judge a person that walks into an office with facial jewelry. Times are changing and a lot more office settings are becoming more lax in their dress etiquette but don't give them any reason to underestimate you. Also, if you have tattoos, try to cover them as much as possible.

When it comes to excessive jewelry and tattoos, the same principles apply to women as well. In terms of clothing, a business suit, sensible shoes (cleaned and polished) appropriate for an office environment, make-up on point and nail polish discrete or non-existent, while hair is tidy.

All the preparations related to the appearance are a must in this process, but having the right information will ensure high performance. Find out everything about the company, such as core activities, history, philosophy and perhaps small financial data (turnover, profits, etc.). Google the company name for any related news articles and utilize Glassdoor for company ratings and reviews. This will help you understand what type of company you are about to walk into if it's reliable, and successful, or has a questionable history with a bad reputation.

Also, make sure you have the correct address of the company or location where the interview is being held. Plan your route accordingly. Make sure that you arrive early, as being punctual is your first opportunity to make a good impression. If the location is not clear, contact your interviewer and ask for the best directions and if there is parking. Don't be ashamed, it only confirms your interest in the position.

Next, you will need to find out everything you can about the position you are interviewing for. The post or ad will provide you with basic information, but you should do your homework to understand more than that. You will need to establish the period of the contract if it's undetermined, whether it's an hourly, salary, full-time or part-time position. If it's not clear, and even if it's plainly listed you should still find out more during the interview. This way you can find out about any benefits, perks, or insurance available to you if you were to join the staff.

When you have all these aspects covered, you only need to focus on the interview itself. Therefore you will need to rehearse on answering the questions you are expecting until you are feeling confident enough for the interview. It's OK to feel anxious before the meeting, that will slowly fade away with practice. To ace an interview, you need to cover all of the steps mentioned above, and to make it even easier for you, the next chapter will cover the mistakes you need to avoid when interviewing for a job.

Core Competencies to Focus On

No one said it would be easy to prepare for this kind of interview. As a starting point, you will need to discover the main competencies the employer is looking for. Researching the company and the position itself will help you in this situation. However, if you are still confused unclear, these are the main competencies to focus on:

- Enthusiasm
- Decision making
- Conflict resolution
- Getting along with coworkers
- Technical skills or those required for the job
- Leadership qualities
- Flexibility
- Team building
- Verbal communication
- Listening
- Interpersonal skills

With this list, you can come up with any and all possible examples in which you can prove your competency. A good starting point is to brainstorm any possible questions you might get from the interviewer. Hint: You can check the following chapters for these. Behavioral inquiries are applicable for candidates who have enough experience to be able to talk about them. But what happens if you're fresh out of grad school? How do you go through this phase of the interview? Think of school projects or situations from school to come up with relevant examples. Even sports events can be a valid source for such instances.

When you don't have anything to show for in these situations, you still have to think of hypothetical examples. Using the STAR method, can help you compile your own stories. Don't just focus on a positive outcome in your example, as you will be asked for situations with negative results, as interviewers want to find out if you learned something from that experience.

Preparing for these questions doesn't always need to happen just before the interview. You might not stay long at your current job, and sooner or later, you may find yourself searching for another position at a different company. So while still employed, write down any instances at work that stand out to you as soon as they happen, thus preventing it from becoming a distant memory.

Chapter 4: What Mistakes You Need to Avoid

It's often said that the best way to learn is from our mistakes. Therefore, if we have experience that ends poorly, we can learn from it by analyzing what went wrong and its effects. Below you can find a list of the nine most common mistakes during an interview. Now, ask yourself how many have you made? Have you made these mistakes more than once? Ultimately, they can prevent you from getting and keeping the job of your dreams, so let's go through them one-by-one, and better understand why they should be avoided.

Not Doing Your Research

If you ask different hiring managers, most of them would say that candidates don't know enough about the company or even the role they are applying for. It's possible that these people are just not interested in putting in the time, or they are overconfident in their skills. Hiring managers prefer those with initiative, and the best way to prove it is by showing up prepared.

Candidates who research the company's history, philosophy, culture, products, and services, are more likely to succeed during an interview. This proves your interest in the company, that you are taking this opportunity seriously and provide a great start to this early phase of the discussion. You can find a lot of information the company's website with a quick Google search, but you should also save some pertinent questions related to the company and the position for the end of the interview.

Being Late

I can't stress this enough. Being on time for an interview is good, being early is better, and tardiness is not an option. Remember that you are not the only person being interviewed for the position, so if you show up late, you prolong the interview schedule and inconvenience your potential future boss. It can complicate the interview before it even beings, as the attitude of the person you are meeting can shift from pleasantries to a crossed arm greeting. Not good.. In some cases, you may be so qualified the interview is merely a formality, and you just blew your chances of being hired.

The first impression is crucial, so you don't want it to be affected by your late arrival. This is why it's essential to schedule your route correctly, consider traffic, possible delays, or anything that might prevent you from arriving on time. If there's an extraneous situation such as car problems, traffic due to a car accident, or road work, you need to contact your recruiter ASAP and let them know you will be arriving late, or if you can't do the interview. If required, you can ask to reschedule. Still, it's extremely important to communicate effectively with the person you are meeting to keep your chances of getting the job unblemished.

Inappropriate Outfit Choice

Even if there is no guarantee of employment, treat the meeting with maximum professionalism. This means dressing for the occasion properly, not because there is a dress code for interviews, but it will contribute to that good impression. Obviously, you can't show up to an interview wearing a t-shirt and sandals, or appear indecent. I have provided some helpful tips related to clothing for each gender, but it helps to find out how the employees are dressing. Check the company's social media accounts, to find any photos of the employees in-house attire, and you will get a better idea of what's appropriate to wear to an interview.

Not Making Eye Contact

You can tell when a person is honest when he or she looks into your eyes when talking to you. Eyes never lie; this is why people really appreciate eye contact. Don't be intimidated by this fact, no one is studying how your pupil dilates with each question and answer, or. If you look away too much when talking to an interviewer, this can be seen as a sign of lack of uncertainty, or they might think that you are not telling the truth. If you find this difficult, focus on one of the interviewers features such as their nose instead of looking away. Be personable, and relaxed with a smile on your face when speaking.

Using Cliches

How many times have you used such expressions as "I'm a hard-worker," "team-player," "fast learner," or "perfectionist," and so on? These are standard replies when asked, "Tell me about yourself," or "Name your greatest strengths and weaknesses." Even though it can be challenging to answer general questions like these any other way, and your competition is likely thinking the same, don't fall into this trap! You need to stand out, and unremarkable answers won't do that., You want to be remembered as the candidate with outstanding solutions even for these bland questions. Make every answer count, and this strategy will pay off and. When writing your "script" for the general questions, make sure that your answers are different than the common ones, so try to come up with answers that the recruiters have never heard before. They will remember you for this!

Bad Mouthing Your Previous Employer

Regardless of the real reasons for leaving your previous job, you should never say anything negative about a past employer or any of your colleagues. This can make you sound petty and unprofessional. You will be asked about why you left or plan on leaving the company, but instead of harsh criticisms that could be considered bad-mouthing, you can come up with a reasonable, diplomatic and professional explanation. It is not uncommon for interviewers to rule you out for these answers. When asked about why you left or are planning to leave your current position, always focus on career perspectives. Perhaps you didn't have any chances to learn or develop new skills, or you simply don't have any chances to get on a higher position. You need to show that you are grateful for the chances you received from the previous employers, but now it's time to move on to the next phase.

Not Asking Questions

The last part of the interview should be for any questions. Based on the information you gathered when doing your research on the company and position, you should already have some questions prepared. Remember, the interviewers appreciate this time, as it strengthens their belief that you are extremely interested in the position. This is why you need to take advantage of this last part of the interview and make it count. Try to ask pertinent questions related to the position, not what was already discussed during the interview. Also, it's better to avoid questions about benefits (wages, promotions, vacation time, and so on), but more on this in the last chapter.

Phone Use

As strange as it sounds, some millennials really consider going on a smartphone (or texting) as acceptable behavior during an interview. In an age where our smartphones are considered an extra limb meaning we simply can't function without them, but that doesn't mean you can disrespect another person's time. During an interview, the phone should not even be in view. Keep it turned off or on silent (airplane mode is also recommended) in your pocket or bag. You shouldn't have any distractions coming from your phone, as you need to focus on your future.

Lying

Unfortunately, too often do candidates decide to beef up, or lie on their resume and sometimes cover letters, just to get the attention of recruiters. The thing is, if you are lying on your resume, you will have to do it during carry those lies into the interview as well. Most hiring managers are trained on how to reveal lies on a resume. Nothing is more embarrassing than to be called out for fibbing during a job interview. You either need to be extremely prepared, make up your own stories, to make them sound true, to get away with it. However, most of the time, people can't lie all the way through the hiring process, as eventually the lies will be revealed.

Why risk losing this opportunity, or any others in the future with this bad behavior? Be as honest as you can with the things you say and write, because if you are invited to interview it is because of the skills, education, or competency you have mentioned on these submitted pages. The rest is up to you.

Chapter 5: How to Ace a Behavioral Interview

Make each interview count. You don't want to be the one always waiting in the lobby for someone else do you? When applying to the ideal job, you should make the extra effort to impress your interviewers and to get the job. Sometimes, we let our emotions get the best of us or can't adequately express our thoughts and ideas in front of strangers. The job interview is not only about showing off your job-related skills, but it's also a test to control your feelings and emotions, as the recruiter will put pressure on you, but this shouldn't affect you.

The labor market is extremely competitive. For each interview you attend, you should be aware that your competition could be out there in the lobby waiting behind you, and your chances of getting the job won't always be likely. So, how do you stand out from the rest? How will you convince the recruiter that you are the perfect match for the job?

You have read about the most common mistakes done during (or before) an interview, and preparation tips. It's good to talk about past achievements, but don't oversell it! Don't talk endlessly about your previous achievements. You are there to discuss the job and the company, so stick to the relevant skills.

Anxiety

Whether we like it or not, we all get a bit scared when it comes to interviews. It's not a tragedy to have a few nerves, it's good, as they are just a sign your body knows you have something to lose. To overcome this anxiety, preparation is your best bet, with a little positive thinking. This is where you will gain your confidence Try not to think of past interviews where you felt like you flopped or said the wrong thing; it will not do you any good! You have already learned your lesson, now it's time to think of happy thoughts. Don't let "negative you" to take over and mess up your confidence and positive thinking. Just believe that you were asked to interview because of your qualifications. They have an image of you, and now it's up to you to deliver, and exceed their expectations.

Developing a positive self-image is very important. You can achieve almost anything in your life if you can believe in it. This principle applies to the job market, as well. You can get the job if you hold yourself accountable. Through hard work and dedication. It's not just about showing up expecting someone to hand you a job You will have to do a lot more to earn the position. And don't ever think that you are superior to the rest of the candidates, this tricks your mind into thinking you don't have to make any effort to get the job. This type of "wing it" attitude will get you nowhere.

Regardless of how skilled and qualified you are, you still need to prepare for the interview, as you don't know what you are competing against. There might be other candidates who are more skilled than you are, or have the same skills and knowledge. Just think that they are all preparing for the job, so it would be in your disadvantage to skip preparing for this moment, and just go at the interview with the "wing it" attitude.

But let's get back to feelings, as this subchapter is more about them than about preparation. Filling your head with positive ideas, having a positive mindset will help you take control over the interview, so the confident persona comes out and "do its thing." It's essential to have a great start of the interview, as this will boost your morale. To be on the right track you will need to relax and try to speak first, as you will have the opportunity to set the tone of the conversation.

If you are good at your job, you should be good at interviewing for a similar position. However, the biggest obstacle in this situation is yourself, to be more precise, your negative persona. You need to have a can-do attitude and to be a "go-getter" to land any position. Preparation is the antidote for anxiety, as it will help you become more confident and to have a positive mindset. Don't compete against yourself, you should be your biggest cheerleader and preparing ahead of time means taking control of any situation you find yourself.

First Impressions

The first impression will set the course of the interview, so it's no surprise if the interviewers start to open up to you, it means you are making a connection.

You will find yourself almost having a better time than you expected. But what exactly will you need to do to impress (in a positive way) your interviewers?

Be punctual and arrive a few minutes earlier. You don't have to arrive an hour ahead of the scheduled meeting time, but most specialists agree that giving yourself 15 minutes to spare is a sign of professionalism. After you arrive at the location of the interview, make your presence known. Greet the receptionist with a smile on your face, clearly state your name and who you are meeting with. They will likely direct you to the waiting room or take you to interview room.

If you have a few moments before the interviewer(s) arrive this is the time to dispose of any chewing gum or mint, turn off your phone, or put it in silent mode. When they arrive be sure to stand up and greet him or her by their last name offering a firm handshake with a warm smile.

Do You Fit the Ideal Candidate Profile?

When posting a job ad, the recruiters already have the profile of the right candidate in mind. You were asked to interview because you are a match. The interview only confirms that you are the right person for the job. So, you really need to focus on explaining yourself and your background to really cement your position.

If you are not exactly sure if you fit this description look over the original posting to find clues about what the recruiters are looking for.

By selling yourself correctly, you will tick each specification and requirement box for the job profile, as you are already prepared to offer examples and arguments to them. An interview is a conversation between two parties, they aren't trying to scare you, or make you feel bad about yourself or lack of skill in one category so there's nothing to be afraid of. You are also to present yourself, find out more about the company and the work that needs done, while the recruiter gets to know you.

Attitude and Personality

In a situation with multiple well-qualified candidates sometimes recruiters will lean on a tie-breaker when they have difficulty selecting. This tie-breaker may very well be your exceptional attitude and personality that stood out among the rest.

You should be looking to display the right mix of:

- polite and professional
- confident
- interested
- enthusiastic

The tone of your voice or the way you speak can also tell a lot of things about you. If you are using an arrogant and condescending tone, this will not get you far. The other extreme, the too lackadaisical attitude, will not help you either. You can be laid back and still well-mannered with a professional tone.

Confidence is an attribute that you need to project during an interview. When you are speaking naturally out of the experience, and you can quickly provide explanations, you will exude confidence as you are

100% sure of what you are saying. Most jobs will be awarded to a confident candidate, as nobody likes a person who hesitates or needs a lot of management.

When it comes to interest, you need to convince the interviewer that you are not only interested in the job, but excited to start. Make them believe it's the perfect opportunity for you and the position you have been looking for. This is why you need to customize your resume for the position, and why you adapt each cover letter as well. Everything you say or do has to say, "Hey! I want this job!"

Enthusiasm will also score you points. This is just a sign that you are a happy person, excited for the opportunity and happy to even be considered for the position. It also shows you love what you do, and how you are looking forward to passing that enthusiasm on to your work and coworkers team. If you have a sense of humor, use it! Win the recruiters over with laughter when appropriate, and you will have a much easier interview. We know enthusiasm is contagious and will make them open up to you. Use it to your advantage.

Skills and Experience

Your resume and cover letter briefly mention your skills, knowledge, and experience. The interview is about confirming this information in front of the employer. Your resume caught his or her attention, now that you have met, it's time to deliver what you promise.

The main rule, in this case, is NEVER ASSUME. Don't expect the interviewer to be familiar with you based on a couple sheets of paper. You are there for the interview to let them get to know you and discuss your work history in-depth. Expect to answer questions your resume has already covered because you can't assume your interviewer has read it more than once. Instead, you can follow these guidelines below:

- sell yourself well to help the interviewer understand why you are the perfect match for the position
- mention relevant skills and knowledge throughout the interview
- try to reiterate important aspects from your resume

- if you don't brag about yourself, no one else will

Some of the Most Common Behavioral Interview Questions

Having questions in mind when preparing for the behavioral interview is useful, as it can help you write down important information and provide examples for these scenarios. You don't have to write a book, keep your answers short and concise. Usually, two-minutes is more than enough time to effectively answer each question. When compiling your answer, make sure to use the STAR method as this will help you structure your answer the right way.

Since you can't predict every question you are given during this phase of the interview, you can only assume that you will have to answer a few of the following questions:

- "Tell me about a difficult problem you solved. How did you solve the problem." With this question, interviewers are trying to find out more about your problem solving skills. For example, if you are working in tech support or customer service, you can easily come up with such a case. Think of a complicated problem that a customer had, how did you handle the customer's frustration and, most of all, how did you solve the issue. For people working in tech support, they are often in situations when they have to troubleshoot the device to make it work. Perhaps the customer is desperate for help and your other colleagues have tried and failed to fix the issue. However, since you know this, your method proves to be successful, and you manage to fix the issue for the product.

- "Give me an example of a mistake you've made." The interviewer is also looking to find out about a situation when you made a mistake and what you learned from that experience. Self-criticism is not always easy, and no one is perfect. From incorrect information logged, to reporting errors, you can use various examples here.

- "Think about a challenging situation you overcame at your workplace." Short deadlines, prioritizing tasks, delivering a project on time, meeting (or exceeding) the customer requirements, you can have different options, you only need to pick the one you consider most relevant to the position.

- "Give me an example of a new skill you learned. How did you learn, and how did you apply it?" Every recruiter likes to hear you are interested in professional development; that's why they are so crazy about candidates who are constantly learning and developing their skills. Whether you are taking a course on new software, or even attending classes at a university to get a degree, these topics are music to their ears. They are very curious to find out how you implement your new skills, so you will need to be very explicit and spare no detail.

- "Have you made any suggestions to a manager or senior leader? What was the result?" In this case, the interviewers would like to find out if you have initiative and provide examples. If you had the opportunity to suggest a different method or approach on how to deal with a customer, make sure to talk about these situations. The interviewers are also looking to understand the relationship you had with superiors.

- "Give me an example of a time when you had to overcome conflict at work." You can write about a disagreement you had with a colleague on what went wrong with a customer. Talk about how you confronted him or her, listened to his/her opinion, provided yours, which eventually led to providing a proper explanation for the client. In other words, a situation where you provided the best solution.

- "Explain a particular situation in which you would have handled things a bit differently." This is the kind of question where you can talk about a mistake you made in the past, what was the outcome, and how you would have changed your actions.

- "Give me an example of a stressful situation you have been through, and how did you work under a lot of pressure." Resistance to stress is one of the key qualities of an employee, even though some jobs don't mention the full extent of the requirements. If you want to prove your point, give an example of when you were you were behind schedule with a project, and you found a way to pull the team together and made your deadline.

- "Can you tell me about a goal you have achieved and how long it took to achieve it?" The fun part about behavioral questions is that no answer is the same. Recruiters really just want to find out about you, how you dealt with different situations, what were your actions, and the outcome. When they are asking about career goals, you can mention a new skill that you have learned and how long it took to master it. If you are interviewing for a position in software development, you can mention a programming language that you mastered after X months or years. You can almost adapt to any situation for this question.

- "Can you tell me about your proudest professional achievement? Why does this one stand out?" Everybody needs to have something to brag about, any achievement that made them proud. If you are at the beginning of your career, you can mention an accomplishment from school. Even if you are working in a fast-food chain, you can still be proud of being an employee of the month. If you sort through your career, you are sure to find a proud moment, but chances are you already have your mindset on one. You only need to explain why this was the achievement you are so proud of. The interviewer only wants to find out how you think, and there are no wrong answers.

Emotional Intelligence

Emotional intelligence (EQ) is an important quality that is overlooked by those in the workplace. However, not many people can honestly say they know something about it. Probably a complete definition of Emotional Intelligence would say that it represents the ability to identify and manage human emotions, but also the emotions of others, to distinguish and label them appropriately. The term was first mentioned in the 1960's by some scholars from Columbia University (Joel Robert Davitz and

Michael Beldoch), but it became a lot more popular in the 1990's with the research of Peter Salovey and John D. Mayer. As it happens, EQ can guide your thinking and behavior and it covers three different skills:

- the ability to discover and name human emotions (emotional awareness)
- applying them to different tasks like problem-solving or thinking
- manage emotions, including adjusting your own emotions and helping others do the same.

Unlike IQ, where there are proven measurements, EQ is found through more subjective methods and is something you develop with time. You will likely be subjected to tests that measure emotional intelligence in the recruitment process. Some people have natural talents such as calmness or patience, and acquire more as they get older. EQ can apply to anything from academic achievement to daily decision-making. According to professionals, there are five components of emotional intelligence:

1) **Self-awareness** is the ability to understand and acknowledge your own emotions. This component is responsible for making you

aware of your actions, moods, but also of the emotions and feelings of other people. To become self-aware, you will not only need to recognize different emotional reactions, but also accurately understand each one. Mastering this component will make you capable of knowing the link between people's behavior and what they are feeling. Self-awareness can help you understand your strengths and limitations, while at the same time provide new information and experiences, helping you learn more from your interactions. People with self-awareness have a good sense of humor, are aware of how other people see them, and they are very confident in their abilities.

2) **Self-regulation** represents the ability to control and regulate your own emotions. The second component of emotional intelligence makes you aware of the impact you have on others, but also supports in self-awareness. You will need to understand that self-regulation should not be about hiding your feelings. This is not a healthy way to manage, control, and regulate your emotions. In plain words, self-

regulation represents the art of expressing your feelings healthily. If you are wondering how mastering self-regulation can change your life, notice that people with this skill are more flexible and more adaptable to change. They are very good at defusing difficult or tense situations, or managing conflicts. Some specialists consider that people with higher self-regulation skills have a more developed conscience, are responsible for their actions, while also being considerate of how they influence others.

3) **Social skills** is considered the third dimension of emotional intelligence, and a very important set of skills that everyone should possess. Also known as interpersonal skills, they are about injecting your feelings into daily communication and interactions with other people. Regardless of if you are making new friends, or just having a conversation with someone you know, social skills will always play a vital role. Managers build connections and relationships with their employees, while the employees develop a strong rapport with

their colleagues, supervisors, or managers. You can easily include verbal and nonverbal communication, active listening, leadership, or persuasiveness.

4) **Empathy** is the fourth dimension of emotional intelligence. It can be considered a special gift, as it involves understanding how others are feeling. If you think that empathy assumes recognition of the feelings and emotions of others, you couldn't be more wrong. Empathy is also about knowing how to react or respond to their feelings. For example, if you notice a colleague is exceptionally sad, this will influence how you interact with this colleague. You might think about treating them with special care or concern, and on top of that, you might make an effort to lift their spirits. Empathy plays a very important role in a corporate environment, as it can help you understand the power dynamics that influence social relationships. In other words, empathetic people will easily recognize who has the power in different relationships, but they can also understand how these forces affect behavior.

Plus, this person can adequately interpret situations impacted by these power dynamics.

5) **Motivation** is very important to EQ, and it has a more fundamental approach. This is the driving force behind success. A motivated person is are very committed, and take the initiative when necessary. If you think that emotionally intelligent people are only motivated by money, fame, or recognition, think again. They prefer to fulfill their inner needs and goals, so they seek activities that bring them personal reward. These people are more action-oriented, and when the goal is set, they have a higher obligation to get it done. They are continuously looking for the best method to achieve success.

Benefits of Emotional Intelligence

By now, you are aware of how emotional intelligence can be useful. With a quick internet search you will find that employees with high EQ are on average more successful than others, and they are more likely to advance in any career. There was a study conducted by the University of Queensland (Australia) showing that people with low EQ and job performance can match their colleagues with better results (better performance and EQ), just by improving this set of skills.

These studies have shown that 90% of the subjects have both high EQ and performance, but just 20% of the low performance people are also emotionally intelligent. Therefore, there are small chances for people with low EQ to have high performances, so people with higher EQ tend to be better at their jobs. As it turns out, the people with high EQ earn with $29,000 per year more than the others with low EQ. The study was conducted in Australia, but it can apply to the rest of the word. (Bradberry & Greaves, 2009)

As every aspect of a business depends on the level of emotional intelligence of its employees, be aware that recruiters are considering this aspect in the interview, perhaps just as much as the others skills and qualifications they are looking for. If you are extremely competent and qualified, try to improve yourself in the emotional intelligence side as well. You will quickly see how well it will serve you in your career.

If you are a bit reluctant about developing this site, then you better take a look over the benefits of applying emotional intelligence. These benefits are divided into four different categories:

- teamwork
- leadership skills
- conversation skills
- people skills

Let's go through each type to understand the advantages of emotional intelligence better.

Teamwork

Companies bring together diverse groups full of different opinions, temperaments, principles, and goals. So, disagreements are a natural occurrence. Who handles these situations the best? The high person with high EQ. This quality enables team members to learn how to manage and control their reactions when interacting with other team members. This can lead to better cooperation within the team, allowing it to become dynamic and more productive. Emotional intelligent people can achieve all of this by increasing self-awareness and regulation, but also the sense of empathy when they are dealing with other colleagues. Getting nothing but the best from your emotional intelligence skills and applying to real-life situations within a company will have a very positive impact on the success of the team and the company itself.

Management and leadership are not synonyms. Managers are capable of assigning tasks, making sure they are done within a timeframe, but they can lack motivational or inspirational skills. However, leaders can easily deal with stressful and difficult situations, overcome conflicts, inspire and motivate other team members to collaborate a lot better in order to achieve the team's goals. Unfortunately, not all managers are considered leaders, so their teams can be subjected to regular conflict. Emotional intelligence can have a significant contribution to better management and better results of the team. Emotional intelligence will help managers to lead by example, and whey they work alongside with the other team members, everything can be monitored a lot better and the employees are also more motivated to work. It's all about winning the respect and appreciation of the employees, and there is no better way to achieve this than being involved in every process. Hence there will be better results if everyone contribute on the tasks (including the manager) to maximize the results of the team.

If you work in difficult conditions, and on top of that, you have low morale, it is apparent for each person on the team. This creates a vicious cycle of negativity among team members. One of the best methods is by creating a can-do environment that encourages a positive attitude. There is no place for negativity and humiliation among the members of the team. The team can achieve the best results as long as every member truly believes that the goals can be reached. People working in sales are very familiar with ambitious targets, but they are not afraid of these targets, and they truly believe the targets can be achieved with the right mindset, attitude and approach.

As a team leader, you will need to know how to bring life and energy back into the group to lift the spirits of the employees. Find new ways to pump them up, and always encourage a positive outlook. Change can start anytime as long as you develop trust, respect, and understanding.

A team can't function effectively without trust, so this is a necessary ingredient to achieve the team's goals and to become more productive. Every high-performing team has a common goal, and most likely, there isn't any team capable of developing trust if they can't work for a common goal. Every high-performing team has a performance-oriented leader, who sets a challenging goal and knows exactly how to handle conflict. When there is trust, respect comes naturally. When team members respect each other, the team as a whole will succeed.

Leadership Skills

Emotional intelligence is extremely relevant when it comes to leadership skills as they play an essential role in:

- Managing difficult situations successfully
- Expressing difficult situations openly
- Becoming respected by their team members and being able to influence them
- Keeping calm when working under pressure
- Leading other team members (or other employees) through a meeting
- Inspiring and motivating other team members to complete tasks

- Staying positive in stressful situations

Emotional intelligence can prove to be extremely useful when inspiring and mobilizing employees to work together to achieve a specific goal. There can be cases when the manager is a very qualified person, but it still lacks leadership skills, as they are not able to get the best out of his employees. When the team is led by a person unfit to be a leader, those goals will not be achieved. You have seen this plenty of times, when workers lack the motivation to put in extra effort. They are doing the bare minimum, just to get a paycheck at the end of the week. This can cause work to stall, and decreased productivity.

Adapting to each team member is yet another thing that emotional intelligence can help you with. It enables you to manage relationships differently and in a more positive way, allowing you to build strong relationships with each team member. Besides being very qualified and competent, emotional intelligence can prove to be decisive when it comes to bringing cohesion to the team, and a better relationships between leaders and each member of the group.

Conversation Skills

Have you ever been in an unpleasant situation when the person you were speaking to was annoying, verbally abusive, or even insulting? If so, did you keep your calm? People working in customer service know what that means, as these are their biggest challenges. We are not robots, and people can get under our skin and mess up an entire day. We all have those situations when we snap, or lose control because of overwhelming anger, stress, or frustration.

You probably admire a few colleagues for their ability to keep calm no matter what the situation. If you are wondering how they do it, it could be for a multitude of personal reasons but they all have one thing in common and that is emotional intelligence. People with this skill set generally handle negative feedback a lot easier, they don't take things personally and won't engage when the person is looking to escalate the situation. These people understand other people's point of view and process negative emotions in a healthier way.

When you are emotionally intelligent, you can easily admit when you are wrong. We all make mistakes, as is our human nature, but only a few of us can recognize when we are wrong or even apologize. Having a big ego will not allow you to see the mistake you made, so you would likely never admit fault. People with higher emotional intelligence are the exact opposite, as they can acknowledge their limitations and weaknesses, and are not ashamed to apologize for a mistake they made. Since they are focusing on becoming better people, emotionally intelligent people are open when it comes to their weak points.

Patience is a virtue, but so is calmness. People have this talent will remain patient and calm, even if they are dealing with stubborn or annoying people. Since they can easily control their emotions, erupting like a volcano or snapping is unlikely. Emotionally intelligent people are also masters of understanding emotion and using this to their advantage. In a disagreement, people with higher EQ can easily convince their opponent to compromise and calm down the situation.

People Skills
Your words don't sound empty when they are backed-up by your feelings and emotions, right? Since social skills represent the third dimension of Emotional

Intelligence, you can only imagine their importance when it comes to expressing your feelings and emotions in your daily communication or interaction with others. In other words, Emotional intelligence can be decisive for improving social skills, especially for:

- persuasion
- communication
- conflict management
- leadership
- change management
- building rapport
- cooperation and collaboration

To have a great performance during your interview, you might want to take a second look above, to understand how EQ can play a decisive role in getting the job, but also becoming successful in your career.

Chapter 6: Q&A On The Candidate's Past Experience and About the Position

How many times have you searched online for the most common questions to expect during an interview? Anyone who wants to do well in an interview is going to consider this search at least once. Sadly, this list won't include a lot of questions structured around your past experience, interacting with others, personality or career growth. I have created these questions for you here to help with that upcoming behavioral interview.

"Tell me about yourself"

It may sound like a general question, but you would be surprised how many people answer this question wrong. The interviewer would like to know more about your educational background and work experience, and you need to combine your answers with some of your skills. Start with presenting yourself, mention who you are, what you have done previously, and what you are doing at the moment. To answer this question properly, you will need to include all information while keeping it under two minutes. Don't fall into a long drawn out monologue about yourself as most people will stop listening, sometimes without even realizing, and that's not ideal in this setting. Keep it short, concise and to the point.

Tip: your answer should not be longer than a page or approximately 500 words. Try writing down your answer, polish it, and make it more appealing.

"Why are you leaving your current job?" or "Why did you leave your last job?"

This could be an employer trying to "push your buttons," and test your reaction. You already mentioned your current or former job in the first question, now comes the dirt. Interviewers will want to know if there were any problems at your last or current job, and issues that can appear again. Don't fall into the trap of providing an answer that might lead them to the conclusion that the issue is you.

Only mention the reasons favorable to you. Don't ever say anything bad about your previous employers or colleagues or put the blame on them, as the recruiter will get the impression that it can happen again with them, and this is a major setback. The answer to this question can be very difficult when you were fired from your last job, so you will have to find a way to spin a termination into a positive answer. The ideal answer in this case is when the company has some financial difficulties and had to let people go, so the company's decision to fire you was not a reflection on your performance. It's very difficult to twist the answer into a positive one for you, if you were fired for poor performance or indiscipline. You need to have a very solid reason for underperforming or for having a lack of discipline. If it was alcohol or drug abuse, you need to convince them that you have overcome your addiction.

"What did you dislike about your last job?"

This can be a complementary question to the previous. Although you've probably had some disagreements with your superiors or colleagues in the past, you shouldn't mention any of this when compiling your answer to this question. The atmosphere at work is never a valid reason, but you can mention something related to career development. Perhaps you didn't have the opportunity to grow from a professional point of view, there was no room to grow or for lateral movement, or you just want to learn and do more, and you felt like the previous place was not the proper environment to take your career one step further. All of these answers can be valid options for this question, so you only need to pick the one that best applies to you.

"What are your weaknesses?"

Expect this to come up at any time, and have an answer prepared. Self-criticism can be very hard, especially when your ego is in the way. The real goal, in this case, is to acknowledge our weaknesses and flaws and express your ability to work intensively on overcoming them. Interviewers will appreciate a candid approach when telling them your faults and will get the impression that you are always trying to improve.

"I see a lot of your jobs have been short term. Why is that?"

This is another tricky question related to your past work experience. Having a resume that shows plenty of jobs, most of them being short term can give the impression that you leave your job very easily.

Obviously, this doesn't look good on a resume, and it's not professional at all, raising a few red flags in the eyes of the recruiters. However, if you can come up with a plausible explanation for this issue, you can still win the recruiters on your side. There are a few answers that will keep you on course to get the job. Mentioning reasons like returning to school, a summer abroad, part-time work, or a project-based position will spark up a new route for conversation. You will have to assure the people standing in front of you that these reasons won't apply here, and you are looking for a long-term collaboration.

"Can you explain the gaps in your employment?"

Depending on the resume format you are providing, recruiters will notice any gaps or extended periods in with no applicable work in your employment history. The scenario is similar to the previous question, so go into detail on how you spent that time away and make it sound good. resent reasons that prove you were filling the gaps with productive activities. If you want to impress interviewers, mention volunteer work, if any, going back to college, or taking courses to get certified in a certain field. If you mention that you love to work, and having some gaps in your employment history is a misleading reflection, you are sure to score some honesty points in this case. Convince them that if given the job, you are committed 100 percent.

"Why should we hire you?"

This is the moment you want to shine, so you bring your A-game. You were asked to interview because of your qualifications. Skills, knowledge, and experience are very relevant for the position, and the interviewer wants to know more. There is a good chance you will get this question, so you should write down your answer ahead of time. Mention your relevant work experience, skills, and knowledge, tell your interviewers that you are familiar with the tasks required of the position, or at least have experience with similar ones. You love your work and you are good at it. Finish with an example that proves how qualified and competent you are in this field. And don't forget to touch on why you are the perfect match.

Picture the same question, but when you don't have enough experience or any experience at all for this position. When recruiters schedule an interview, even though you don't have the required experience for the position, it's because they see potential in you. This is the reason why you don't have to disappoint them and answer this question in a manner that will leave them speechless. Perhaps some companies are fed up with so-called experienced candidates who will turn out to be disappointing when it comes time to apply their skills and knowledge. These companies prefer to hire a college grad or a person with no experience at all, train rigorously, so they can mold the candidate they need. If experience does not matter in this case, perhaps your educational background could make a difference, even a course to learn and develop new skills can prove to be very useful.

There are plenty of people interested in changing their careers, just because they don't like what they are doing, or are not paid enough for their service. A candidate looking to switch his or her career can be highly regarded by the recruiters, especially if they can prove during the interview that they have the basic knowledge to start this job, but with an emphasis on their willingness to learn and go through intensive training. The salary might be lower than the ones of a qualified employee, so you can use this to your advantage, as some companies prefer to pay a lower wage in the beginning, but invest money and time in your training. Perhaps this question is asked at an interview for an intern position. You need to compensate for your lack of experience, with enthusiasm and willingness to learn.

"Where do you see yourself in 5 years?"

Showing too much ambition, may not be wise in this case. Perhaps the recruiters are looking for someone to remain in the same position for many years, so showing career advancement intentions may not work for you in this case. However, playing the stability card, may be exactly what they want to hear, but does this represent your best interest? what you can do in this case is to come up with a compromise between ambition and stability. The interviewer is interested in finding out whether you are serious enough to remain in the company but would like to find out if you have given some thought about your career development. If you have goals related to the position you just applied, make sure you mention them to the interviewer. If the position you applied for is not related to your career goals, you will need to mention why do you think getting more work experience in this position is part of your career plan.

"Name three of your biggest professional achievements."

If you don't have anything under your belt this can prove to be a very complicated question. And replying with "I don't have any major professional achievements" will not help you Scan your work history, even back to high school or college, if necessary, to come up with compelling examples of professional achievements. Whether it's a student exchange program, being part of a highly productive team, or being named "Employee of the month" when working in a local fast-food restaurant. Even these achievements matter, so don't underestimate them when it comes to this question. If you don't have anything from your career to brag about, perhaps back in school or college, things were a bit different. You can be the captain of the debate team (this can matter a lot), or perhaps you won some prizes during a school competition. Everyone can have something to be proud of, so now it's the moment to mention these achievements or accomplishments.

"Describe your biggest challenge of your professional career."

When you have responsibilities, it's only a matter of time until you will be facing different challenges, more or less difficult. In fact, having a lot of difficulty can only lead to healthier career development. In this case, the best thing to do is to mention a very relevant challenge to the position you applied for. If you applied for a customer support position, then you have to mention a situation when you had to handle a very frustrated and abusive customer. Describe the situation in detail, make sure you mention your contribution to the whole situation, how you handled the customer, how you were a calming presence, or you managed to provide a satisfactory service in the face of uncertainty. It's important to come up with an example that has a positive outcome, as the employer will want to know if you are capable of handling these situations and still coming out on top. Depending on your experience and the position you applied for, you can pick an example that will make them remember you. This is the kind of question for which you will need to reply using the STAR method, so write down your answer and make every word count.

"Can you provide an example of a task you have done so well, that it exceeded the expectations of your clients?"

It's important to meet the requirements of your customers, but to exceed their expectations will make you ace in their book. If you are a software developer, for instance, you can mention a particular project that left your customers speechless. They were amazed by the app design and how smooth the interface is. It can be an example of a perfect product that won respect and appreciation of your clients.

"Can you think of an example when you had to handle a very high volume of tasks? How did you prioritize them?"

This scenario is becoming very frequent nowadays, as you are probably left to cover for a colleague who went on vacation, and you have twice the work to do. Also, when we are talking about a very busy period, these situations are also common. There is a chance that you have been through these situations before, and you only have to remember how you handled them. Perhaps all of these tasks are more or less urgent, and you may be required to work overtime to make sure they are done on time. You need to emphasize that you are first prioritizing tasks according to their priority level and getting to work. You may mention about staying late or coming earlier to make sure these tasks are delivered on time. This can show commitment, ability to work under pressure, but also knowing how to prioritize tasks.

"Please describe your last project."

If you are more focused on taking project-based jobs, then there are high chances to receive this question. This question applies to freelancers, the ones focusing on living one project to the next, or for professionals like graphic designers or software developers. In this case, you will need to mention your client, what is his domain of activity, and what was the project. You can then move on to details like project requirements, the tasks you had done for the project, and the result (the customer's opinion about it). This question could prove to be very useful for you if the project was relevant to the position you applied.

Tip: Regardless of what happened with your last project, you need to present everything from a positive point of view.

"Have you ever been fired?"

This can prove to be a tough question, but keep in mind that recruiters can get references from your previous employers, so really need to be honest when answering this question. If you have experienced this before, you still need to find a way to present the situation in a positive light. Perhaps there was the restructuring, and the decision to let you go had nothing to do with your work performance. If the decision was influenced by your lack of discipline or poor work performance, explain the circumstances of your actions and emphasize that it will never happen again. The purpose of the question is to find out if the candidate can acknowledge his or her past mistakes and prove that you have learned from these experiences. It's up to you to present a negative situation positively. Imagine delivering a hard message to someone, but you need to use your soft skills to do it right and minimize the blow back. That applies in this case.

"What are your salary expectations?"

There are plenty of cases when the salary is not mentioned in the job description when the ad is posted. This leads to additional research on your part as you will need to find out what is the salary level for such a position, according to your experience. The number you will get probably doesn't match the one the company is willing to offer, but at least by doing this research, you can find a range in which most likely the salary offered by the company will be included. People are often unsure how to answer this question. In such cases, candidates can leave it up to the company representatives to offer a fair payment according to your experience and qualifications. If the recruiter insists on hearing a value, you can provide a salary range that will be satisfactory for you. You can also provide reasons to back up your requests, but those reasons should always be about your skills and knowledge, not personal reasons (e.g., you have a high mortgage to pay, higher monthly expenses, and so on). When you are providing the salary range, you might want to go high, as recruiters will only consider the lowest value from that range.

"Tell me about the biggest change you had to handle in a previous job."

In this case, the interviewers are trying to find out how easy you can adapt to different situations, how flexible you are. They are trying to discover how you react when you are taken out of your comfort zone.

You need to come up with a valid example of this situation. You can talk about a change of plans when delivering a project. For instance, if you are working in marketing or sales, the results of the marketing strategies have to be measured. If they are way below the expectations, then the strategy needs to be adjusted. You can mention such a change for this question, but don't forget to mention how you adapted to the change, or if the change was effective.

"Give an example of a situation when you failed to communicate appropriately. What would you have done differently?"

You don't have to think too hard to come up with an example, as these scenarios only happen a few times. I'm talking about the situations when you are misunderstood, especially when you are dealing with customers. To give you an example, a customer can ask for more information on a product you sell. The product may sound like a great deal, but you soon discover that it's not suitable for this particular customer, as the product only applies for new customers (and he/she is an existing one). In this case, it led to a misunderstanding, and providing all the required details for the customer should have been done before creating any confusion.

"Can you provide an example of developing an unconventional approach to solving a problem?"

Describe how you developed this approach and what challenges you faced. Let's say you have a customer that purchased the wrong product because the one they were looking for was out of stock. The refund process takes a while, the customer is frustrated and wants their money back immediately. Instead, you place an order for the original item they were looking for to be delivered to their home. You even manage to get it at a discounted price. The customer is satisfied and provides you with great feedback. Luckily for you, there wasn't anything stopping you from providing this solution. This question refers to creativity, and how the unconventional approach might be the right one.

"Please provide an example when you had to change your approach in the middle of the project."

The answer you can provide to this question can be related to the question about the biggest change you had to deal with. Think about a project where things were going in the wrong direction and you didn't realize until it was almost complete, so you and your colleagues had to change approach to get the project on the right course. It can be a project (a phone app for instance) that you worked on, and when it was very close to the due date, you realized that the app is not working as it should be. Luckily the testing phase can easily show you where the mistakes are, so you can adjust them fast enough for the app to be fully functional before the due date.

"Think about a situation when you had to perform a task you had never performed before"

One of the best ways to learn a new skill is when we have a need for it. When you are faced with a task that you have never performed before, it's better to ask more experienced colleagues or try to find out more info on how to do it or use the internet as an infinite source of information. At least this is what I would do and how I would answer this question. Again, the software developing world can come up with some of the best examples. Your client may want some functionalities and features that you have never applied before, but you have a slight idea how they can be fixed with a technology you heard about. Therefore, you learn more about that technology and find out everything there is to know about it in order to apply it to your project.

"Please describe a situation when you failed to meet the customer's expectations. Think about what happened, and how did you try to change the situation."

When you are working in a field challenging as customer service, these situations can happen quite frequently. You might be willing to help the customer, but the company policies will not allow you to provide the solution the customer is looking for. Companies need to handle their customers with care, but this doesn't mean that every customer request has to be satisfied. Some of these customers are too demanding, and they are "phishing" to get something they are not entitled to. When they find out that the product or service they want isn't free of charge at a considerable discount, a switch flips and they are disappointed and frustrated with the service the company is providing.

A golden rule and something to always keep in mind with customer service is that you can't win them all, so do your best, but you won't always be able to satisfy every request from your customer. Instead, you need to find a way to deliver a negative answer in a positive light. Learn how to develop your positive language skills and use them, as you will notice, they make life on the clock a lot easier.

Let's say that you have a customer complaining about a technical malfunction he experienced with a product sold by your company. Everything is fine now, but he doesn't want a "faulty product" and demands a full refund in cash on a credit card purchase. The issue was never reported by this customer, but he still insists on receiving compensation. He is frustrated and starts using abusive language. Although the company policy clearly specifies that a refund can't be offered, only store credit, and certainly not cash with this transaction. The best way to handle this situation is to find out more about the technical problems, and give the customer the impression that you are doing your best to understand the issue so he can enjoy his purchase. Or get in touch with your manager on duty, and kindly explain why you don't have the permission or authorization for a refund, he may have gotten more frustrated and annoyed. Keep your calm and let your manager step in, as these kinds of situations can lead to a complaint against you. Your manager will take the case and provide a hard message to him, and you can rest assured that you have done everything in your power to provide high-quality customer service within the company policy limits.

"Can you think of an example when you made sure that the customer was pleased with your service?"

This is yet another question that sales and customer service reps can relate to. Sweetening the deal is a practice that people working in these fields can do to get great feedback, and also win the customer's loyalty. If you treat your customers like royalty, they will definitely appreciate it, reward your efforts with excellent feedback, make recommendations to their friends to come see you for more orders in the near future.

If you are working for an online store, and a customer claims that he purchased your products by mistake, he apologizes for the inconvenience, and he is very nice and calm over the phone, this is the kind of customer worth being helped. Your company already provided a refund for the customer, under the claim of child purchase, but this time the situation is a bit different. He doesn't have high hopes of getting his issue solved, but you know you can help him from the beginning. It's important how you sell this option to this customer. Always give the customer the impression that you are doing your best to help him, but you are a bit skeptical when it comes to his chances of getting a refund.

Tell him that you need to get approval for this refund, and get back to him as soon as you can with the good news that you 'somehow' managed to obtain a full refund for him. You can make it sound like you went the extra mile for the refund, or this is a very special exception that you are making for him. The customer will highly appreciate this (apparently) extra effort, and you will win his loyalty, provide you the best feedback, and get you extra recommendations.

"Can you think of a successful presentation that you had at a previous job?"

If you applied for a sales or marketing position, you should expect interviewers to ask this question. It can be a presentation you held during a conference, where you have a massive audience. In this case, you need to spare no detail, as you will need to mention the product or service you were talking about, where was the presentation held, your target audience, but also feedback after your presentation and an outcome (you received more requests for the product or service, different people were more curious about it, and they were asking for additional information about it).

Such an example can only prove that you are an extraordinary speaker, and your words have a high impact on the audience. It can also confirm your excellent persuasive and presenting skills, and they can serve you well in this situation. Think about Steve Jobs and his presentations of the newer versions of the iPhone, its new features and functions. Think of the impact it has on the consumers and on the massive queues for buying the latest iPhone. Obviously, this is just an example, you can get your inspiration from, but no recruiter will believe that you held such a high impact presentation with such a massive audience.

Your example can be of a smaller presentation, where you had twenty people or so in attendance. It could be about the service that you are selling or promoting, like software or insurance, so you need to point out the advantages, benefits, and client eligibility. Your audience can be formed of interested individuals from all different levels, and after your presentation many of them are interested in finding out more about your product, service, or placing an order.

Questions About the Position

"What do you know about X position?"

Some recruiters may have a very different interviewing style compared to the standard one. Usually, they are starting to present the company and the job, but some interviewers want to know what you got from the job description and the position itself. This is where your research comes in. You will need to know the job description almost memorized, but don't rely on it. Going through job descriptions for similar positions can also be very helpful. All this information should help you provide a very good and informative answer.

"What do you know about the company?"

Following the same principle above, you could also be asked this question. Your research on the company has to be very comprehensive and shouldn't rely just on the company website. You need to find everything there is to know or can be found about the company's history, philosophy, all its services, and products, and financial details if possible. Of course, you don't need to tell them their company's turnover, profit, or loss. However, if you know all these details, you can come up with an answer that will surprise the interviewers in a very positive way.

"How can your skills help our organization to grow, increase revenue, and produce results?"

Here you will need to focus on your strengths and relevant skills for the organization. If your performance can be measured through KPIs, then you need to provide specific examples from the past when your skills and experience made the difference and helped the company perform better. If you are applying for a customer service position, you can explain how your calmness, patience, and strong communication skills can be regarded as a valuable asset for the company. Your answer should project confidence and enthusiasm; otherwise, it will not be adequately received.

"What would you do better or differently for your company?"

This is yet another question when comprehensive research pays off. You already know a lot of information about the company and the position, information that you can use to your advantage. If you add your most valuable and relevant skills, then the answer will be astonishing. If you are applying for a sales or marketing position, you can suggest a different sales or marketing strategy, but you need to back it up with arguments. If the position is about customer service, then you can suggest a different approach that you know from your own experience that pays off. This question is all about making a difference. Do you have what it takes to make a difference?

"How long do you think it will take you to fully perform?"

The interviewer might ask you this question because he or she would like to know how long it will take before you can fully operate on your own, without the help of colleagues. The answer you will depend on your experience, but also on how fast you are learning during the training process. In countries around the world, the probation period may be different depending on their labor legislation. In the US, this probation period lasts for 90 days. Sometimes that is how long a training program will be and it's your time to shine. After these 90 days, they will have an idea if you are a match or if they need to reassess your position. So make sure to fully commit.

"What expectations do you have from this position?"

You could be asked this question as the recruiters would want to avoid seeing any disappointment on your side, just because the job is not what you expected. This goes way beyond the job description, as the tasks mentioned will be handled by you. However, this question is more about career growth and promotion possibilities. If a candidate expects to be promoted after one or two years, and that isn't likely, you will see the employee become demotivated, underperform and probably leave. If you have expectations of a higher salary after a fixed period, after having great results, but the company doesn't meet your expectations, then you probably need to keep this to yourself. Mentioning anything about salary and benefits so soon is considered unprofessional. The company representatives will know how to win the loyalty of their employees and reward them according to their performances. Have no fear and clearly state your expectations from this position, whether you want to develop new skills, or get promoted to a higher position, etc.

"Are you willing to relocate?"

Moving from one location to another can be very difficult, but you shouldn't be kept in a place where you don't have any career possibilities. Most companies still prefer old-fashioned work from the office, meaning that you will need to go to a designated located where the company is located. Most managers prefer this method of working, as they have higher control over the employees. When the company representatives are asking if you are willing to relocate, you need to do some calculations, as relocating will probably mean paying a higher rent. Assuming that you already know the salary range for the position you applied for, you can easily decide if this decision can work in your best interest. Some people are fans of telecommuting, but this can lead to high transportation costs, so depending on your current financial status this may not be in your best interest. However, when asked if you are willing to relocate, you need to think where you have better opportunities. Taking this into consideration will help you make the right decision. Some companies can allow working remotely, which can prove to be a great choice for you. But this is something that you will need to ask the interviewer.

"Are you willing to work nights or weekends? Overtime?"

Working past office hours or over the weekend can be a deal-breaker for some, but many are in a position to work long hours and extra days. Extra dollars on the paycheck each week is a motivator to stretch yourself too thin sometimes. It's up to you if you can or want to work during these periods, some positions may require you to work weekends or nights based on rotating shifts. This means you might have to work weekends twice a month, or nights one week per month. Usually, these conditions are mentioned in the job description so they shouldn't come as a shock to you. By applying to the position you are more or less agreeing to the conditions mentioned in the job description.

Chapter 7: Questions About Interacting with Others

Most managers would consider that the interest of the team should prevail in the personal interest of an employee. Therefore, every member will need to pull together to achieve the best results. Cohesion plays an important role, as it can lead to a productive collaboration between every team member. Perhaps, this is why team-building activities are so popular within companies. An interviewer considers this to be of high importance, so not only are they looking for the candidate with the best job-related skills, but also for the one that can easily blend in with an already existing team.

"What irritates you about co-workers?"

The team brings together people with different beliefs, principles, or personalities, and it takes an outstanding leader to make the team work as one When you are fully dedicated and do a great job, but you other colleagues of yours not being too involved, this might get you frustrated. Whether the team performs very well, and they are taking advantage of these performances by receiving the same bonus as you (although they don't deserve), or it's just the other way around when the results of your team are affected by the lack of dedication coming from these colleagues of yours, then you have all the right to feel that way.

"Are you a team player?"

This is just one of the questions that you will receive most likely. Answering "yes" will not cut it. The best answer to this question is to provide a very relevant example of teamwork in which you were involved. I'm not referring to winning a little league baseball game. You will need examples from your professional career. From working as a crew member in a fast-food restaurant to having a group project in which you were involved (applies for software development), there are countless examples you can provide in this situation. Just remember to use the STAR method and spare no detail about the situation, your contribution, and how it impacted the result.

"What kind of person you would refuse to work with?"

The answer to this question can be taken from the previous one related to irritating co-workers. If you are doing all the work, while you are not receiving any help from a colleague, or they don't offer any contribution but you share the credit. You can't work like this. The person who doesn't get involved, and lets you do all the work is just an example of someone you should avoid. If your colleague is not qualified or competent enough, and you have to help them over and over again, and you have to explain what to do each time, then you should let your superiors know what's happening. There is a type of colleague with inappropriate behavior that should not be applied anywhere. I'm talking about the abusive colleague, whether he or she is verbally abusive or even sexually inappropriate. Under no circumstances should you feel you have to work with this person. They should be reported to HR immediately.

"What your previous supervisor would say about you?"

How you see yourself is one thing, but how others are seeing you may be the exact opposite. To have a good perception of reality, you will need to understand what others think of you, especially when it comes to managers or supervisors. You can't read minds, but if you had a very good relationship with your previous manager, and you left in a friendly manner, you can only assume what he or she thinks of you. It wouldn't be wrong to brag a bit about your qualities and skills in this case. Mention only a few of your biggest strengths, but try to keep it short.

"Tell me about a problem you had with your previous manager?"

Not all people are the same, as they might have different opinions, beliefs, and principles. Therefore, having disagreements seems to be something natural in a team with different types of people. But what happens when you disagree with your manager? Answering this question can prove to be extremely difficult. Some people comply with everything the manager says so they don't get in trouble. Someone may have a strong personality, and when they experience a difference of opinion, they like to express it, even if it leads to a disagreement or a fight with their supervisor. The best answer would be an example of a debate you had with your manager about how you handled a customer. They might argue that you were too generous to the client, so you explain the reason and logic behind your actions. Using a calm tone, you managed to avoid escalating this conversation into a full-scale blow out over this topic.

"Do you prefer to work individually or within a team?"

There is no wrong answer to this question, and let me tell you why. Working on your own can say a lot of things, like independence, confidence, and being fully prepared. You are committed to doing your job, you will focus on your tasks, and you are interested in doing a great job. There's nothing wrong with that. This kind of attitude is specific to salespeople. However, there is nothing wrong with preferring to work in teams. Common goals are easier to achieve if all the members of the team work together. Most of the time, supervisors prefer you to put the interests of the team first, and yours second. The ideal answer to this question is, in fact, a combination of both: individual and teamwork. Do you know why? Because a team will have the best results when every individual wants to outperform themselves.

"Have you ever made a decision that you knew certain people would not accept? Please

describe the decision-making process and how did you handle the reaction."

This question can only apply if you previously had a management position. When you have such a position, your decisions can be very unpopular to some of your employees. Whether we are talking about a bonus (some people feel like they are left out, although you know they don't deserve a bonus), or asking some people to work late because someone is on vacation, and their work needs covering. You can't please them all as a manager, but you only need to care about the interest of the team, not the interest of certain individuals. If confronted by these people, you can explain your decision to them, to make them calm.

"Can you think of a situation when a colleague asked you to do something, and you objected? How did you handle the whole situation?"

Think of a scenario when a colleague of yours asked for help after the multiple times you spent your time helping them. You are getting fed up with the requests and you think they don't know how to do their job, so you refuse. In this situation, you need to explain your decision and why you are not willing to help anymore.

As an alternative, encourage them to learn on their own time.

"Describe a situation in which you played a decisive role in improving a team's performance. What were the challenges you faced, and how did you address them?"

Interviewers are big fans of leadership skills and this question is the perfect opportunity to prove your leadership skills. If you had a project in which your contribution improved the overall team performance, don't hesitate to mention such an example.

"Think of a situation when you and your colleagues were not getting along. How would you handle such a situation?"

Perhaps you have already been through such an experience, and, in this case, you can answer a lot easier to this question. But if you haven't been in such a situation, you can think of a hypothetical case like a team sport. Let's say that you and your teammates are not working together in one particular game, which is out of the ordinary for you, and you are losing. You need to explain the importance of working together and collaborating to see better results. Also, by appealing to their ego ("We can't let them win, they are not better than us"), you can bring them together and start acting as a team, not just like a group of people with no connection or relationship whatsoever.

"What negative thing would your last supervisor/manager say about you?"

This question is more about how you think others are seeing from their perspective, especially the perspective of your former boss. You can answer this question if you think about the relationship you had with him or her. Did you have any disagreements or did they appreciate you? If you were the kind of employee who could set a positive example, then you probably have no clue how to answer this question. However, there is always room for improvement. Perhaps, the most common answer to this question would be: "He/she was not satisfied with how I handled a project or a customer," so to handle customers with extra care or to pay more attention to project details, meetings or very important emails is perhaps the best answer in this scenario.

Chapter 8: What Questions You Can Expect Related to Career Development

Career growth is something you always need to focus on, although there are candidates who are "settlers," who are pleased with their tasks and don't want to aim for more. You are the only one responsible for setting your career goals, so it's up to you how high you want to climb the corporate ladder. Recruiters like ambitious people, but if you are not feeling confident about how you should approach these questions, perhaps it's safer to find the middle ground between stability and ambition. To answer these questions professionally, you might want to take a look below, as you will find out how to respond to some fascinating questions.

"Describe your ideal job."

When you talk about your ideal job, you need to think of what you truly love to do, what are the tasks that you enjoy the most. In this case, you will have to explain that the job you applied for is the job of your dreams. Focus on your strengths and the tasks required for the position. Convince the recruiters that the job you applied to represents the opportunity you've been looking for. Don't waste their time by answering that the ideal job pays a lot for minimum work. You are disqualifying yourself with this answer.

"Are you currently involved in other recruitment processes?"

You will need to be honest in this situation, so if you are scheduled for an interview at another company, it is better to mention it. Talk about having alternatives to choose from, but emphasize why you prefer this position. If you lie and deny that you are involved in other recruitment processes, you might find yourself in an unpleasant situation when you are contacted to be offered the position, but you have to refuse it as you already accepted another job offer. This shouldn't be possible if you were not interviewing for other positions, so this can have serious consequences for you. If you are in this situation, you can consider that you burned all the bridges with this company. If you apply again to this position, chances are you will not be considered again. This is why you should mention if you are attending other interviews. This is not to put pressure on them, just to give them an honest answer about your current status.

"What are your short-term goals?"

You have to be prepared for this question, as there are high chances of getting it during an interview. Although some people like to think they can advance very fast, and the reality is not so glamorous. Your career has to be built on sustainable pillars, and you need to learn a lot of new skills to improve them; otherwise, these pillars will collapse, and your career will go with it. A sustainable career is built with baby steps, not in fast-forward. Therefore, it's better to answer that your short-term goals are to gather as much knowledge as you can, to learn and develop new skills, to become better at doing your job.

"What are your long-term jobs?"

Don't hesitate to display your ambition, as this is what the recruiters really want to hear. It's OK to mention that you are only interested in learning and developing new skills. State your career ambitions clearly, or how high you want to climb the corporate ladder. If you are applying for a junior accountant position, it's natural to mention that you see yourself as chief accountant, or the CFO in a major corporation (in more than ten years). Depending on your starting point, or the career path that you choose, you can mention the position you are trying to reach. Some people will probably want to take the entrepreneur path after a few years of working in a company. Make sure that your plans for the future are ambitious enough when answering this question. Also, since this question is very common, you might want to write down your answer when preparing for the interview. Polish it, make it more appealing, as you want this answer to stand out from the rest.

"Please describe how this position can help you with your future career?"

To properly answer this question, you will need to point out that all your previous experiences have been very useful for your career growth. Applying to this position doesn't make any exception, as you can see great potential in this work environment. Make sure you mention that you like to make the most from each position you work, as you are building your career on the skills you learn from each job. Answering this question will also reveal your expectations from this position. Explain what skills you think you will learn and develop from this position, and how you will benefit from them in the long run.

"How long do you plan to stay with us?"

Investing in an employee can be very consuming in terms of time and money. An employer may provide the training for you, and even might have to pay to get you qualified and prepared for the job. It will be considered a loss if the employee leaves just a few months, right after he or she has been trained and qualified for the position. This is seen as a betrayal by the employer, as the employee didn't stay long enough to make up for the money the company invested in him or her. The recruiters are very interested in finding out how long are you planning to stay with the company. If you weren't asked about your career ambitions, it's wise to mention them now. If they can be satisfied with this company, then point this out. In this case, it's ideal to find a middle ground between ambition and stability. As long as the company can provide you the conditions to learn, grow, and possibly even get promoted, then you see no reason to leave the company.

"How will your personal life affect your performance at work?"

Although most recruiters will choose not to intrude in your personal life, there might be a few who will be very curious about this aspect. You may be asked if you are married or if you have any children, but the discussion typically stops there, as they don't want to get too personal. However, there might be rare occasions when recruiters want to find out how your family will affect your work. Perhaps you have to take your kid from school or kindergarten, to bring it to work for an hour or two, or your wife has just given birth. As you can imagine, all these aspects may affect you when it comes to work, as you may need a more flexible schedule, or perhaps you are not getting enough sleep to be in your best shape at work. Perhaps you may have to telecommute for a longer distance, as your family doesn't live very close to work and you have to be with them every day. Regardless of the condition or issue you have related to your personal life, you need to be honest and mention it, as recruiters are entitled to know this information about you if they will offer you the position.

"Are you available to travel?"

Some positions may require a lot more dedication and commitment than others, so that they might require some traveling for business. There are plenty of candidates who love to travel and to attend business meetings, but it all depends on their availability. People working in sales are out of the office at least half of their work schedule, meeting different customers. You need to ask yourself if you are open to traveling for company purposes, and how often. This is a sacrifice that you are making, as you will be away from your family and friends for a certain period. Perhaps this is what you really want, as nothing pleases you more (from a professional point of view) than these delegations. These business trips will have a higher value in your resume, but as mentioned above, it can have an impact on your personal life. You need to know what you are giving up and what you are gaining if you choose to often go on business trips. If you are not married and don't have any kids of your own, then please mention how much you love traveling and how much you would benefit from this opportunity. If you are married and have young kids, perhaps it's better to mention your limited availability.

"What is more important to you: money or work?"

The problem with the young generation is that they are extremely material and they focus too much on getting more money. If you ask any millennial what their motivation is, almost all of them will say money. In other words, they would easily leave a job for another one, if the other position offers a higher compensation. These people don't care about learning and developing new skills, and even if they are working in a place where they can grow from the career perspective, they can still leave the position for a better paid one at another company, where they probably don't have opportunities to grow. Recruiters don't want to hear that you value money more than your job itself. So, if you want to get the interviewer on your side, you need to mention that your job is more important to you than money. A good explanation would be that a higher salary level can be sustained only by higher level skills. Therefore, you focus more on getting new skills, then on getting a higher salary. If you have a higher salary, but you don't deserve the salary, as you are not qualified for the position, most likely you will not remain in the same position for long. When this happens, you have minimum chances of getting another job with the same salary level. However, if you have more skills to back up your salary, you will be a lot more protected, as it will be easier to keep your job, or in the unlikely event of a company going bankrupt and letting people go, you will have an easier time finding another job for the same or better pay.

"Can you tell me about a time when you set a goal for yourself? Have you achieved this goal, or you are still working on it?"

By answering this question, you are stating your ambitions related to career growth and professional development. It doesn't have to be only about getting the job of your dreams, it can also be about learning skills you want to someday master and grow from a professional point of view. Remember, for your position to be sustainable, it has to be backed up by hard work, and high skill levels required. Otherwise, you will not be in that position for a long time. Some people want to learn software development because they think they need a career change, and this domain offers a very high salary or hourly wages. Others would like to run a business of their own, so they attend a business school, or even an MBA program, to learn, grow, and develop the best managerial skills. Perhaps you can find yourself in this scenario, but the important thing is to set a goal related to developing new skills, but you also need to set a deadline for it.

Most people are willing to make a change and to become better at what they are currently doing, or to learn something else. The motivation behind new skills can be, in most situations, getting a higher income, as we tend to spend more, even the money we don't have. Make sure you mention any of your career plans when it comes to learning, and be aware that you can only stop learning when you retire. You can adjust your goal to different scenarios and relate them to a hobby or a long term goal you want to see achieved. Perhaps you decide to start training for a marathon, and you want to be able to easily accomplish the distance in a good time frame within the next four months.

Chapter 9: Tricky and Common Questions About The Candidate's Personality

The profile of the ideal candidate is not just a sum of technical and soft skills, otherwise there would be no need for an in-person interview. There is still one ingredient required to have the ideal candidate. I'm talking about personality. If all the other questions are designed to find out if you are a competent candidate for the position, or if you can blend in the team, the recruiters are also interested in finding as much information as they can about your personality. In many cases, these recruiters have at least a little psychological background, and are very good at finding hidden details about your inner self. If you are applying for a position within the Secret Service working for the President of the U.S., then most likely, this part would be very important and comprehensive. However, for regular jobs in the private sector, you really can't expect to get too many questions related to your personality, and most of the questions you will get you can find below:

"Tell me a little about your personal life"

Don't see this question as an attempt to reveal your intimacy, as this is another chance where you can shine and come up with an answer that can impress your interviewer. If you are good at story-telling, then you need to use this skill to your advantage. Everybody loves a good story, so why not present the story of your life. Add a bit of humor to it to win them over. You might be tempted to start a long story, but this is not the time. Try to keep your answer within 2 minutes, make it short and concise, and cover all the important facts from your personal life. Make the story more interesting and appealing, just like a sales pitch story. Have you ever checked the story or a video of a crowdfunding campaign. This is the ingredient that empathizes the wide audience and makes them donate to a cause. Your story doesn't have to sound tragic, as you are not there to make your recruiters feel pity about you, but it should be inspiring and attractive enough, just to make them remember you.

"What are your hobbies?"

You were asked to interview so the company representatives can get to know you better. Asking about your hobbies can tell a lot about yourself, more than you can imagine. There are no wrong answers here, unless your hobbies are related to addictive and degrading activities, like gambling, social media or watching Netflix all day. Everybody likes to hear about interesting hobbies like reading books (you might be asked about a favorite book or author), traveling, hiking, playing sports or just spending quality time with your friends, family or kids. You can simply adjust the answer that you will be giving to best describe you as a person. If you are telling about reading books, learning new skills (you are probably trying to learn as much as you can about software development), or watching some documentaries, these hobbies can only show that you are a curious person who is constantly focusing on learning new things.

If you mention spending quality time with your friends, going out (to make more friends), playing sports, these hobbies can prove that you are a very social person. Also, if you are a part-time freelancer, doing graphic design, developing software, translating or just writing articles, it's to mention these activities as well. It shows that you prefer to stay active during your free time and do something productive. Therefore, try to come up with an answer that will make you look very good in the eyes of the recruiters.

"Name one word that best describes you."

This answer doesn't have to be too elaborate, but in this case, you really need to think of your best strength and character trait. Think about that one word that can sum up what you really are. You really don't have to mention any of your weaknesses in this case, as you have the chance to put yourself in a positive light. So, don't waste this opportunity!

"Do you consider yourself a big-picture person or a detail-oriented person?"

This might sound difficult, but if you are thinking it through, you can really come up with a good answer for it. The big picture-person is the more innovative person, who can come up with ideas to perform better. As you might think, this is the profile of the visionary, who is more suited for a leading role in an organization. The detail-oriented person is the perfectionist type, the meticulous and comprehensive planner. No detail gets passed him or her, and it's the kind of person that knows his or her way around huge amounts of data and numbers. So, how would you describe yourself, bearing in mind that there is no wrong answer. You need to explain why you see yourself as a big-picture person or a detail-oriented one.

"How would you rate your professional experience?"

It's fine to brag a bit about your experience, competences and skills, but try not to create a false image of yourself, because if you are being hired you need to deliver what you promised, otherwise you will not be in that position for long. Try to be as objective as you can, as recruiters already have an idea about your competences, skills and experiences, and being honest in this situation can score you some points. If you are deliberately underestimating your professional experience, this strategy can also prove to be a winning one, as it shows that you are not satisfied with the level you have achieved, and you are looking to grow a lot more. Regardless of how you would rate your skills and experience, it always helps to explain your answer to the people standing in front of you.

"How do you handle stress?"

Stress resilience is one of the most appreciated qualities in work environment, as there are plenty of jobs having in their description at requirements "resistant to stress" or "working well under pressure." You need to elaborate and provide a very relevant example. Just think of the STAR method as you might need to write down your answer. Even though the question doesn't specifically asks for an example, the best way to answer it, is to provide an example. So, what exactly can cause you stress? Is it your monthly expenses, loans or mortgage? Try not to get to personal when answering this question, as the interviewer doesn't want to know about your debts, and how well you can perform under these circumstances. You will need to find stress factors from your work environment, whether you are talking about handling urgent tasks with a very strict deadline, or you are dealing with a very demanding customer that really wants to get a very special service from you. Both of these scenarios are valid and can be mentioned in your answer, so think of a complicated situation, a really stressful one, what were your actions, and what was the end result. Nothing can prove more your stress resilience than a very relevant example.

"If you were to restart your career, what would you do differently?"

There are plenty of people who are having a career switch at one point in their professional experience, but you are not trying to explain why you would like to take a different career path. You want to get the position you applied for, not to change your career. If you really want to come up with the right answer, you need to think of what you wanted to become when you were a kid. If you mix your answer with a sense of humor, you can also win them over. Just to give you an example, let's say that you wanted to become a doctor when you were a kid (perhaps one of your parents is a doctor, or you have somebody in the family doing this job). During school, you even liked Biology and you even had very good results. Now, you are probably regretting about not going to Medical School to become a doctor. You went instead to Business School, as you are more passionate about Finance and Accounting. Expressing your regret about not following the medical career will probably be the wisest answer in this case. Sure, you had to spend more years studying, but if you compare the salaries, it still pays off, right?

"How would you evaluate success?"

Recruiters want you to be successful in this position. This is the reason why, they need to understand exactly how do you see success. Do you consider it can come from talent and skills, or do you think success can be achieved only through experience, hard work and dedication. If you are thinking that success is a combination of both, then you are right. This is the perfect opportunity to list the ingredients of success, but also to motivate your answer. Unless you are extremely lucky, you can't achieve success only through talent and skills. You have to achieve it the hard way, through hard work and dedication, but using your skills and talent to help you along the way. Having great results is what success is about, but keep in mind that there is always room for improvement. If you want to preserve to state of success, you always have to aim higher and to perform better every day. When you set the bar high, not only that you constantly need to reach it, but you also have to lift it higher.

"Can you think of an example when you had to think outside the box?"

This question brings your creativity and ingenuity to discussion, so you might need to dig deeper in your professional career to provide a valid answer for this question. It can be a situation when you had to provide an alternative solution for a customer, as the standard solution may not be in the customer's best interest. Discovering the loophole in the company policies, may allow you to come up with a brilliant solution to the customer's needs or issues. It can be a solution that nobody else thought of.

How to Answer Any Question in an Interview

In addition to applying the STAR method when compiling your answers, make sure that you follow the principles below when answering these questions:

- Be concise: Most likely you are not the only person being interviewed that day, and the recruiters are time-limited when it comes to interviewing you. He or she would like to cover the questions planned, so your answers will have to be concise. Even if you like to talk a lot, keep your answers short. Provide examples, and back-up every statement. Describe the situation, explain how you handled it, and never forget to mention about the results. Examples will help you to provide succinct and on topic answers.

- Never place blame on a previous boss or staff. As you can see from the questions we answered in this book, you may have to describe difficult situations that might not have a positive outcome for you. In this case, you will need to take full responsibility for what happened and to explain what have you learned from such an experience. These questions are about you, not about your previous manager or colleagues, so leave them out of it by not placing the blame on them.

To sum-up, always remember the tips below, as they can help you have a great performance during the interview:

- Be an enthusiast as it can be infectious. You can easily change the mood of your interviewer with this attitude. Plus, if you also have a sense of humor, you can use it in order to create a positive atmosphere.
- Project confidence with every word you say. Sell yourself in a confident and professional manner. Never leave the impression that you hesitate answering any question. This can come from your preparation, as you don't have to be very spontaneous to ace an interview.
- Make sure you mention all your relevant skills, knowledge and experience. You can't leave anything to chance, and most of all, NEVER ASSUME that the interviewer already knows about your skills and experience. The recruiter will not know if you are not telling him or her.
- Express your interest in the position with every word you say, your body language and your reactions.

Chapter 10: It's Your Turn to Ask

The final part of the interview is dedicated to you, as you will have the chance to ask some questions to your interviewer. Assuming that you had an outstanding performance during the interview, you merely have to make this section your "grand finale." If you have already proved your enthusiasm, confidence, professionalism, and interest for the job, during this section you will prove that you are properly prepared for this position and you are taking the job opportunity seriously.

By doing it the right way, you will make sure to cover everything. Closing the interview, should be another time when you shine so don't miss this opportunity, after all, every word you say during the interview can make a difference, therefore you will need to make any question count in this phase. If you are truly prepared you already have a few questions in mind, but make sure that during the interview the answers to your questions were not already given.

Although it's very indicated to ask your interviewers a few questions, try not to hold them up for too long and save some questions for the next time you meet. Specialists would agree that having up to five questions is more than enough for this part of the interview. But before you ask any of these questions, make sure your key strengths relevant to the position were covered and if not, you can mention them now.

If you are wondering about the questions you can ask them at the end of the interview, I've compiled this list for you:

- "How many people there are on the team?"
- "Who will I be reporting to?"
- "What kind of training will I receive?" This shows that you are curious about the support the company will provide you in order to perform properly on the new position.
- "Can you be more specific about the duties I will have?" This is when you still have some unclear things about the job description.
- "How will the position develop?" You are looking to find out about the career prospects of your potential new position. The answer

should cover aspects like potential new skills and tasks.

- Ask about the nature of the industry. You might be interested to find out if the domain of activity is dynamic, stable or complex, plus you can hear about how the company is compared to its competition.
- "How are priority assignments handled within the company?" In this case, you want to find out if management asks you to fulfill higher priority tasks, or if you decide on your own.
- "How do you see the company/department changing in two years?" You are curious about getting more information regarding the company development for the upcoming years.
- "Is it possible to show me the office where I will be working?" There are some occasions when the interviewer can give a tour of the company, including showing the office where you will be working. However, if the recruiter is not doing this voluntarily, you can also ask about it, most of the time they will give a small tour of the company, including your future workstation or office.

- "When do you need someone to start working on this position?" In this case, you can also mention the date when you will be available.
- "Can you describe a normal work day here?"
- "Is it possible to go through training a bit faster?" This question shows that you are looking forward to starting working on the position ASAP.
- "How much contact is there with manager and superiors?" You will find out how the communication process works between you or your future colleagues from that department, and superiors/managers.
- "Am I transferred between functional fields during training?" In this scenario, you would like to find out if the training you will be receiving covers different tasks, just to know the company better, or the product itself.
- "Is travel normally expected?"
- "How soon can I be advanced to the next level?" This prove your interest in career growth, so you are displaying it one last time during the interview.

- "How often can I expect to receive a performance review?" You are aware that you will have the extra attention of the management, so you need to excel at everything that you are doing. Although you need to constantly work to improve your performance, it's good to know when the performance reviews are being done.
- "Is it possible to receive decision-making authority after one year in this position?" You would like to find out if your responsibilities will grow over time in this position, to an extent where you can take decisions on how to perform your tasks.
- "Does the company offer any educational benefits?" If you want to prove that you are a person interested in learning, then this is a great question.
- "Are there any new product lines/services announced recently?"
- "Do you relocate employees?"
- "What is the working schedule?"
- "Are there any options for a flexible schedule?" Asking questions about the work schedule can

only show one more time the interest you have in the position

- "Are there any possibilities to work remotely?" Some companies can allow this option when some of their employees are leaving far away from the office. Being stuck for 2 hours in traffic when you are going to work and returning from it may be very time consuming, and you are not left with any spare time to enjoy with your family. Asking about "work from home" opportunities can change your life.

Choosing three to five questions from the ones mentioned above should be more than enough in this situation. However, try to avoid asking questions about salary, vacation or benefits. Indeed, this information is extremely important, but you will need to wait until you are offered the position.

However, these questions should not be the final ones coming from you. When you are about to leave the room, make sure you thank the interviewer for taking the time to see you and mention that you look forward to hearing from them. Don't forget to ask the following question: "When you are looking to make a decision regarding this position?"

Of course, this question you will ask if they don't mention anything about how long the interviews will take, so if they don't provide you a time estimate, it's right to ask about it. The most important thing about your attitude during the interview is to always have an optimistic mood. Regardless of what the interviewer is saying (or not saying), never let yourself be discouraged. This applies also when you feel the interview is going in the wrong direction, you feel that have been rejected already, or in the discussion, the topic of pay was never mentioned. You have to keep your energy up no matter what's happening in the interview room.

Conclusion

Most of us are not willing to take the risks that come with choosing the entrepreneurship path, so they are more keen on building their own career as a simple employee. Challenges and temptations can be found at each step of a career, and these reasons determine whether a person changes their job more frequently than our parents did. If you look at your parents resume, you will see most likely just one or a few jobs, and this can only mean that there was a lot more stability back then, than it is nowadays.

The corporate lifestyle involves fierce competition, tight deadlines, stress, and multitasking. Things aren't what they used to be a few decades ago, there is a high emphasis on productivity, efficiency, and, most of all, profit. For the sake of profit, companies are letting people go regardless of their work performance. The labor market has never been more competitive and finding the job of your dreams can be a lot more complicated than you think. It seems like people are only looking after their best interests, and they really don't want to settle for one career. Constantly changing jobs and switching careers has become a natural occurrence, so when you are applying for a position, you are not only competing against the unemployed but also skilled and experienced candidates who just want a different job.

There are plenty of ads out there that have tens, if not hundreds of applicants, so if you want to stand out from the rest, you need to start with your resume and cover letter. These documents will have to point out your skills, knowledge and experience relevant to the position you applied for. You need to customize each resume that you send out when applying for jobs, as recruiters will need to understand you want to apply for this position, not just a job. Your cover letter should briefly explain why you are the perfect match for the position, and having the best-looking resume that is structured and packed with important information will get the attention of the hiring manager.

The recruiters will shortlist the candidates according to the resume and cover letter of those who match the job profile. If you are among the shortlisted candidates, congratulations, you have passed the first round of the recruitment process. The next phase will be the pre-interview discussion over the phone. This will be a short interview that can still rule you out from the process, so it's not the first interview, and you will automatically pass to the next interview. To narrow down the number of candidates, recruiters can use this method, but can also apply tests if the number of candidates is high.

When it comes to the interview, most likely, the recruiters will have between 5 to 10 other candidates. Therefore, if you made it to this phase of the recruitment process, kudos to you, as you probably manage to eliminate other tens or even hundreds of candidates. As this will be your first physical interaction with the company representatives (and hopefully not the last one), you will need to use every ace up your sleeve to impress the company representatives.

It's important to arrive a few minutes before the interview. Make sure you have enough time to eat, go over your resume once more and plan your route so nothing will prevent you from being on time. Look amazing, and pay extra attention to your clothing and grooming. Greeting everyone from the receptionist to the interviewers with a friendly smile on your face can make a huge impact. Your body language during the interview will be observed by the recruiter, so be careful how you gesture, how you hold your legs and hands, and also if you are a bit more boisterous, you should be aware of your reactions.

The best way to prepare for your interview is to anticipate the questions you will be receiving, and how to answer them. Practice out loud, just like an actor rehearses for a role. If you properly prepare for your interview, you will become more confident and a lot less anxious. This book provided you with a wide range of examples of questions you might get during an interview. Whether you want to find out more general questions, but also behavioral questions on different categories, you need to go through this book, as it can provide you answers or tips on how to answer these questions. Every behavioral question should be answered using the STAR method, as this the default structuring method for these answers. These behavioral questions are all about examples, so you need to spare no details when answering them. Even if you are tempted to provide a long story, you need to keep it short and concise, so your answer should be less than two minutes.

If you are tempted to blame your previous boss or your colleagues for your failures, just don't. This is not very professional and really doesn't look good in the eyes of the recruiters. Be a responsible candidate and take the full blame for the negative results you had. Explain what you learned from your mistakes and assure the interviewer it will not happen again.

Throughout the interview, you will need to keep up your enthusiasm and a positive mindset. Regardless of their reactions to your answers, or if you feel that the interview has gone south, you remain the same. However, if you want to impress the recruiters, you will need to go through the chapters of this book, find out the questions and answers that you will receive most likely, but also to find the best tips and tricks to ace this interview.

As a fair disclaimer, this book will not guarantee you the job of your dreams, but it will definitely minimize the number of interviews you need to get the position you have always wanted. Be your biggest cheerleader, even if you fail! Never let yourself down. Always use turn failure into a lesson to learn, improve, and eventually have enough experience to share your knowledge with others. Happy job hunting!

If you found this book useful in any way, a review on Amazon is always appreciated!

www.ingramcontent.com/pod-product-compliance
Lightning Source LLC
Chambersburg PA
CBHW030651220526
45463CB00005B/1726